Hearts of Faith

Hearts of Faith

Bonnie Brockett Kuhn

Copyright © 2013 by Bonnie Kuhn Events

Hearts of Faith by Bonnie Brockett Kuhn
Cover and Book Design by Bonnie Brockett Kuhn

Printed in the United States of America
Requests for permission to make copies of any part of this book can be made to:
Bonnie Kuhn Events
P. O. Box 3210
Arnold, CA 95223 USA
www.bonniekuhnevents.com
First Edition 2013

ISBN-10:0615926487
ISBN-13:978-0-615-92648-3

Preface

The poetry within this book, written during the
period 1945 to 1953, reflects the "Old English" style
of writing. These poems are in the exact style,
language, spelling and tone of the authors.

To my family and friends of Justine Brockett.

To every individual who suffers from a chronic disease.

To every caregiver, whose heart and soul are given to care for a loved one

May one day we find solace,
The peace within our souls.
The eradication of disease,
Leaving each of us whole.

~Bonnie Brockett Kuhn

Contents

Introduction

This book is a tribute to Justine Brockett and her mother, Cassandra Hallett.

The poems were found amongst Justine's most meaningful treasures during the period of her final days at home in hospice care with her family. It came to the family's attention that their mother and grandmother had sought God's love to guide them through an extraordinarily difficult period of their life.

Marvin Hallett, husband and father perished during World War II in 1945, at the Battle of the Bulge. Cassandra became chronically ill with Non-Hodgkin's Lymphoma Disease in 1946. In 1947, she was stricken with Tuberculosis. Her illness required that she be quarantined in a facility; leaving her daughter and son in the care of social services. She passed away in 1953.

Due to Cassandra's illness, medical professionals prohibited both Justine and her brother from being with their mother. They spent the remaining period of their mother's life in over 14 foster homes, often separated from each other as well.

These poems, written during 1945 - 1953 followed the death of Marvin and the induced medical separation of Cassandra from her children. Cassandra and Justine simultaneously wrote their thoughts and prayers through poetry unbeknownst to each other.

The poems reflect their search for God's love and the Savior's guidance to overcome the pain, sorrow, angst, hope, loneliness, fear, war, loss, separation and need for connection and support through faith. Justine and Cassandra were able to cope with their losses and separation by knowing and believing in God's divinity and love.

In Loving Memory

Justine Brockett
January 29, 1940 - February 28, 2013

Cassandra Carmela DeBiaso Hallett
1921 - 1953

The faith each shared carried within their souls, guided each one through challenging emotional and physical circumstances. In 1966, Justine was diagnosed with Multiple Sclerosis. It was her continuing faith that empowered her life. Enabling her to live a full life enriched with a devoted husband, loving family and her own special joy of life.

Justine's final days of life were at home in the loving hearts and arms of her family, and with the dedicated nurses and staff of the Hospice of the Sierras, Sonora Regional Medical Center, Sonora, California.

Hearts of Faith

Will You "Hide" on Judgment Day

What will you do on Judgment day?
Hide from the shame and disgrace?
Or, will you purely meet our Savior,
Smiling, face to face?

What will you do when Christ comes again?
Will you shout and clap your hands?
Or, will you try so very hard,
To reach the 'unknown hands'?

If you are not saved, my friend,
Come unto Christ today.
Ner'e has fear of hell or wrath,
On that great Judgment day!

Come unto Christ, my friend,
He died to save us all.
Come unto Christ, my friend,
He saved us from 'The Fall'.

Come unto Christ, my friend,
And, meet Him face to face.
Come unto Christ, my friend,
Finding heavenly grace.

Be Thou Awake!

Sleep not be thou awake,
Sleep not in death, oh friend.
Awake, O' life, freely take,
Sleep not in evil bend.

Sleep not, be thou awake,
Watch and Ye shall see.
The peace and glory for our sake,
Is great beyond all sea.

Sleep not, oh friend, be thou awake,
A Savior, God did send.
Make peace with Him, and Ye shall find,
Life and love, no end.

Forever Christ

Sweet Loving Savior,
Thy love is pure.
Sweet Loving Savior,
Thy way is sure.

Sweet Loving Savior,
How gentle thou are.
Sweet Loving Savior,
My shining star.

Pure, truth and love thou art,
Giving man a fresh new start.
Sweet Loving Savior, from me,
Thou art not apart.

The "Son" Shines Through

When the "Son" shines through.

The waters are smooth.

Not raff and wild and torn.

Your heart finds peace.

Lasting lease, your inner soul reborn.

Deeply you breathe and inhaling deep.

Your world is now at best.

You look not far.

The Morning Star whispers lasting rest.

Pure Love

Savior let not me stray away,
Keep love about me day by day.

Let not mortals take your guard,
Keeping child enclosed Thy yard.

Keep Thy dove upon Thy face,
Teach me "love and heavenly grace."

Let my footsteps follow Thee,
Let Thy hand upon me be.

Let Thy seat thou enclosed,
Be remembered, not reposed.

Heavenly love Thy ways are best,
Safe with Thee, forever blest.

Help Me Overcome Myself!

Oh my God, I need Thee most,
Each day that passes by.
Dear God, my Father, help me see,
The sin that I imply.

Help me go in light each day,
And keep Thy hand upon my brow.
Let me always follow Thee,
Where taste of sin, allows.

Help me keep my spirit clean,
And fall far from evil heeds.
Let me know the good in thoughts,
Action, words and deeds.

Keep me cleansed as well within,
Pure, sweet and loving kind.
Without, let me go about as Thee,
Ner'e let me with man bind.

Keep me close to Thee in pain,
Teach me of my unholiness.

Let me always bind with Thee,
And receive Thy tender kiss.

Let me be strong and walk Thy way,
In any task, I across must come.
Let me always strive in 'Light',
And meet with Thee at home.

With Christ, Thy loving Son.

"Love"

Ever loving, ever near,
Ever gracious, ever dear.

Gifts untold brought forth to Thee,
Always willing, always He.

Forgiving man untold returns, never failing,
Entangled gift, Him I Yearn, God most holy hailing.

"Be not dubious,
For 'tis God calling you.
Be unafraid,
My God is ever true."

God's Christ

Comfort, peace, love Sublime,
Shelter untold, these are mine.

Gracious, loving, tender blends,
Home with God never ends.

Peaceful, hopeful, joyful, glad,
Ever endless, never sad.

Contentment, songs above, beauty expressed,
Always thine, forever Blessed.

Bible

Do you love Him, God our Great?
Do you seek Him, at the Gate?

Do you want, at the end?
Do you know Him, on the bend?

Do you care that He knows you?
Do you want good pathways, too?

Do you dream of Him on High?
Here, there, everywhere, Nigh?

If these things you do want,
Choose to pray and know His want.

These things, all, are in "The Book,"
He has left near the nook.

So you may know what is expected,
Read it now, don't neglect it!

Christ, The Hidden Jade

'Tis force against disastrous foam,
That rebels against the dome.
The goal ahead, ne're let it shed,
But foam alone, ner'e roam.

'Tis stricken death, to disastrous foam,
Air'e turning back the haze.
O' shallow foam put on 'weight'!
Within the hidden glaze.

Let not Thyself be stricken,
On shore, be not afraid.
Thy foam upward trend,
And find the 'Hidden Jade'.

It's color of perfection,
And stone beneath is strong.
Find eternal wisdom,
Against the broken song.

'Tis such beauty held within Thee,
'Tis peace beyond all sea.
'Tis glories' grace, most given,
Disastrous foam, now free!

The Key!

Someday I'll see the castle high,
That few on earth could reach.
The castle few can speak of,
In their Golden Speech.

The castle now, I've key of,
As Christ has given me.
The key, the door to open,
The castle of Eternity.

Rest My Weariness

Oh God, rest my weariness,
And give me peace of mind.
Let not me fuet the material world,
In Thee, let me be kind.

Keep my soul cleansed, pure snow,
Keep my heart as fresh as dew.
Oh God, let not me fuet with fear,
At night, let me be with You!

Close my eyes, let sleep appear,
Let not me toil in thoughtless tear.
Oh God, keep ever close to me,
Ever, ever near.

Let not me think selfishly,
Let not me dwell in sin.
Oh God, keep me safe with Thee,
Letting Christ come in.

Lead My Doing Work

I need Thy strength, my God most High,
In Thee I am all strong.
No fear can overtake me then,
Nor can I do no wrong.

In Thee 'tis life and lasting power,
In Thee 'tis grace and life supreme.
My heart is light, with Thee, O' God,
My soul is a golden beam.

Oh God, make me always trust Thee,
In times of trying trials.
Let me always look to Thee,
In my humble style.

Oh, God let not me fear this world,
And conquer all for Thee.
Let me live the Golden rule,
And find Thee in Eternity.

Keep Christ within my humble being,
Let the spirit guide me strong.
Forever lead me places clean,
To live the life I long.

Let not my inner self come forth,
'Tis evil that I know!
Lead me God, oh lead me safe,
All the walks I go.

The Father, Son and Spirit

O' Blessed Trinity,
O' Spirit Divine.
Keep ever loving me,
Spirit hail, Divine.

O' Blessed Trinity,
No withered flower be.
O' Blessed Trinity,
Spirit safe, eternally.

O' Blessed Trinity,
Thou art love Sublime.
Father, Son and Spirit, all,
Precious soul, Divine.

O' Blessed Trinity,
Keep me safe with Thee.
O' Blessed Trinity,
In all, eternity.

O' Blessed Trinity,
Let me drink Thy Wine.

O' Blessed Trinity,
The Blessed Son doth shine.

O' Blessed Trinity,
Thou art my lasting life.
O' Blessed Trinity,
Safe in Thee, no strife.

As far as the East is from the West,
I pray my faith stands fast.
As far as the South is from the North,
Dear God, my love away not cast.

Christ, The Hand

Mysteriously, a hand sprung up,
Lifting O' the weight.
Elated t'was the feeling,
From my stricken fate.

O' t'was good, the peace now gained,
O' burden air'e t'was great.
But, mysteriously, the hand came forward,
This loving Hand of fate.

It reached within my depted soul,
And softly called my name.
Often it had dealt with me,
When once I was in 'flame'.

O' that Hand of all such goodness,
I bend before Ye, pray.
Ne're let me go in blindness,
'Mysteriously', guide my way.

Christ Alone

Sooth my aching bones O' Lord,
For weak I be, 'tis true.
Teach me purity and love, Lord,
That truth known to the 'few'.

God, give me everlasting love,
Ne're let me cruelly be.
Open wide 'that heart' Lord,
That Thou dids't give to me.

Let me see about me,
Those in love, and those in despair.
Let me always kindly deal,
To folks I meet, everywhere.

Let me go 'bout in Thy grace,
And let me never fail to pray.
Keep Thy love about me,
Ne're let me become fray!

Guide my every secret thought,
In pureness let me speak.

Ne're let it be the material wealth,
About me here, to seek.

Let me know the value,
Of this gracious, golden fate.
Ne're let me linger unwisely,
Ne're fear that hand of Hate.

Come to Me "Open Up Your Hearts"

I knocketh, doth thou not hear me?

Open up your hearts and let me in.

I rappest now, wilt not thou let me enter?

I am Jesus, Son of God, who died for sins.

I am come, doth thou not see me?

For I look upon you all with my Great love.

Let me enter in your hearts that I may save you,

Jesus, your lord, who wants
you all with God, above.

I am here to today, "*my loved ones,*"
let me enter.

So you may have peace,
in eternal life with God,

Let the 'door' of your hearts,
now, be opened.

And walk with me,
this Blessed road, to trod.

Open up your soul, your life eternal.

Open up your hearts, and listen now!

Unburden all your cares upon Jesus.

Who died, upon 'The Cross' to save our brow.

My 'Perfect Friend'

For Years I've hunted vainly,
Seeking 'Perfect Friends'.
Finding all disappointments,
Around the many bends.

My heart was sore in seeking,
No peace of mind at all.
The rapture of fulfillment,
Came clear, 'the great stone wall'!

Heartache after heartache,
Time and time again.
My need now more thou ever,
Was for this 'Perfect Friend'.

The many years passed along,
My 'Friend' up not shown.
Yet I kept seeking, seeking forth,
Like many mortals, you have known.

God appeared often in past thoughts,
But He was a' where's beyond.

And yet at times close He felt,
As Father and Son in bond.

And yet I went looking on,
For my 'Perfect Friend'.
I found I prayed to this God,
At every rugged bend.

Now he seemed so near me,
At every nick and nall.
And many times he saved me,
From a drastic fall!

More and more I spoke with Him,
And my seeking ceased.
More and more I trusted Him,
And found my faith increased.

He was then guiding me,
Lifting me above.
Teaching me of Christ, His Son,
Who died to prove His love.

At last, I gave my heart to Him,
And found my 'Perfect Friend'.
'Tis Christ the only Son of God,
In Him life has no end.

I've never known such happiness,
Until finding my 'Perfect Friend'.
For in Him I've found all answers,
Which in the world, I couldn't comprehend!

Life Through His Son

Thou wretched burden, I am,
Thy soul is torn between.
Aching man, Thy self-hearts tortured being,
And the supreme.

Tangible man, rusty form,
Thy days do mourn.

"Shell-flesh" mortal,
Wrapped in carnal.

'Lax and patient be,
Man, not man, only God can see!

Lifting weights and measures,
Sublimness full treasure.

God's Gift and measure, His Son.

God's Portal

Passion greater, spirit lingers,
Holding close within one's fingers.

Drooping petals, loves' dying breath,
Shielded from wrath and death.

Unfolded charms within the gleam's,
Laughter, beauty though it seems.

Death, despair now gone,
No withered lily shon.

Man O' Man thou art shattered,
Stepping stones thou art scattered.

Broken bits among the tawn,
Wake up O' man 'The Dawn'!

Breathe freely, take thou 'life',
God's Portal, shun all strife.

'You' Were Calling Me!

O' Father the road was dark and long,
With endless sorrows and tears.
I couldn't see no one but self,
And the world of constant fears.

My thoughts were ones of grief and pain,
My mind beyond repair.
I couldn't see no one but self,
And saw the world in despair.

I suffered so and whined away,
No smile, only gloom.
I only thought of myself,
Away in a lonely room.

T'was one night I began to pray,
'Cause you were call me.
I asked then for courage and strength,
And began to trust in Thee.

You led me then to safety,
You made the way so bright.

And made me to understand,
'Tis Jesus the 'Son' of Light!

It's a glorious feeling,
To know you're always near.
Self-pity overtaken,
When you drove away my fear.

This gift of life I treasure,
For 'tis worth more than the world, all.
To trust in you, O' Father,
In Christ I cannot fall.

It's a glorious feeling,
When, in trying times.
To speak with you, O' my God,
My heart then rings as chimes.

Lord, I have knocked,
And thou has't let me in.
Lord, I have asked,
And thou has't given me.

Lord, I have prayed,
And thou has't known me.
O' Lord thou has't told me all,
And Lord, I believe.

Lord, I have seeked,
And thou has't let me in.
Let me ever do Thine will,
And souls for Thee win.

Christ Rings the Bell

Christ rings the bell for me,
And the music from my soul.
Comes from Christ my Savior,
Who died to prove His goal.

He laid down His very life,
To prove His love for me.
And said, follow straight and steady,
As he'd come back for me.

He proved His love O'er, and O'er and O'er,
This each day I know!
His hand always upon me,
His love a constant glow.

He sets the path for me to go,
Lest I falter and am lost.
For, Christ died to save me,
At a drastic cost!

"Greater love hath no man,"
He laid down His life for me.
Save my soul from Hell and doom,
Place me with Him in eternity.

The 'Light' Found

T'was dark and dreary, that road behind,
T'was ever fearful, ne're t'was kind.

And peace t'was not known, nor had,
Forever, ever sad.

T'was dead and lifeless, numb and cold,
And peace t'was not to hold, O' bold.

Then a 'Light' appeared,
Ne're afeared.

Faint t'was seen the 'Light',
A delicate sight.

At time's t'was blue,
Beyond the que.

But, God gave the soul the strength,
To carry on at length.

Rehearsed, the darkened soul,
Found peace 'n goal.

The 'Light' t'was seen, where shadows bound,
T'was Christ, the soul had found!

Solitude

Wondrous night, love's sweet song,
Sweet dreams ringing clear a throng.
Silent hours, solitude,
These are the wistful longs!

Hold them ever dear to Thee, sweet night,
Of restful peace, love is near.
Longing end where love begins,
Contentment and always dear.

Melt Not Away!

Gently fall the flaky foam,
God sends to men below.
Gently snowy, whitened flakes,
To men on earth they go.

The trickle here and there - beyond,
On Thee and house and road.
Warm and snuggled are the folks,
In homes that they abode.

And Yet 'one's' home is not the earth,
Nor sky, nor sea and lake.
All on earth will pass away,
Look closer through the veil!

Earthly life is as the flake,
For a moment we be here.
The nexed afar we're taken,
Many not knowing where?

And, yet each soul could find the 'home',
That lasts eternally.

For God has chosen all to come,
To abide with He 'safely'.

Like the flakes, he sent men,
In earth to make it clean.
And Yet we sin,
And on ourselves do lean.

When at last we 'melt away',
And dying cry - "Save me God!"
For many, many, many men,
Wonder why this cause!

As the flakes, He sent His Son,
Who died to free them stricken fate.
He loves all with purity,
And releases men from Satin's hate.

In Him, we melt not away,
As the flaky bit of snow.
In Christ we're safe, regardless,
Of places foreign to go.

My Savior Lifted Me

T'was all gloom and darkness 'round me,
Before my Savior lifted me.
T'was all sin and sorrow and sadness,
Christ then came and lifted me.

T'was all pain and fear within me,
Before my Savior lifted me.
T'was all hate and worldly badness,
Before my Savior lifted me.

He changed my world of darkness and sorrow,
Now I know He truly loves me.
Placed all smiles in places of tears,
'Cause He bled and died for me.

Now I know I'm saved from damnation,
'Cause my Savior lives for me.
Now I know someday I'll see Him,
For my Savior waites for me.

His arms are opened, loving, tender,
'Cause my Savior waites for me.
I shall rise to Heaven to glory,
'Cause my Savior lives with me.

Keep My Ship A' Sail

Oh, let the waves beat to and fro,
Against my Iron ship.
And let the rugged waters whip,
Against my strengthen bow.

The mighty hand, the rock, the force,
Upon my iron bow.
Ne're let not me sink below O' Lord,
Ne're turning back my course.

O' God l' not man fail Thee,
Across these waters broad!
A ship without its captain,
Is as a broken rod.

Set the stern a' straightway course,
Keeping all aboard.
Keep that ship a' sailing,
Ne're let it taste remorse.

Lord, let that sail upward trend,
Across these rugged seas,
Set foot at last on solid ground,
With Christ in Eternity.

Can You Keep "Smiling?"

"How can you keep smiling?"
This, often, I am asked.
How can you keep going,
Your face a' fresh, unmasked?

How can you hold your head high?
Ah, a happy sigh...

How do you keep smiling?
I never hear you cry!
You've lost your very loved ones,
Your heart must be, oh, sigh!

And Yet you can keep smiling!
Your strength cometh where?
And in my heart, I smile, 'cause,
Christ is hidden there!

Let Not Pride Take Thy Soul

O' whithered tulip fading 'way,
O' whithered root of longing clay.

Quick and swiftly thou must die,
Hold fast, now, no longer sigh.

Listen close when taking prey,
God will lead to you the way.

Long hang unto phrases known,
For 'tis better than to groan.

Let not the foolish inner pride,
Take away the utmost Guide.

Follow swiftly lest thou fall,
Hasten to the Savior's call.

Ne're letting man taking force,
O' whithered soul take remorse.

Live not in green, O' whithered soul,
Nor letting bondage take control.

O' whithered root of evil force,
Take free life, straightway course.

Let Christ rule, all and all,
Listen to His gentle call.

Proceed

Sometimes man does reveal the things they are,
But only God knows fully what lies within the mar.

Man is futile when going only by man,
But with God, anything he wishes do, he can.

So man, take heed and be not a weed,
For only God can make a man succeed.

Follow Christ Today!

Persist not in sin, O' man,
For the day of wrath and doom.
'Tis near around the corner,
'Tis one of fearful gloom.

Persist not in sin O' man,
Make peace with God today.
Receive eternal life and glory,
On that Judgment day.

Persist not in sin O' man,
Come to Christ, repent.
He payed for all one's wickedness,
He's the Savior our God sent.

Persist not in sin O' man,
Have peace within your heart.
Christ is more than loving, as,
He gives a fresh new start.

Persist not in sin O' man,
Give your heart today.
Follow now in righteousness,
With Christ our Savior, pray.

Sleep Not, O' Friend

Sleep not, be awake,
Sleep not in death, O' friend.
Awake, O' life freely take,
Sleep not in evil bend.

Sleep not, be awake,
Watch and Ye shall see.
The Son of God in all glory,
Waiting for you and me.

Sleep not, O' friend, be awake,
A Savior, God did send.
Make peace with Him and Ye shall find,
Love and life - no end.

Give It Drink!

Give the seed drink, and watch it grow,
Give it thought each day.
Watch the root take hold in clay,
Give it 'drink,' ne're delay.

'Twill break through the soil, a bit at a time,
A tree now e're strong.
Straight and firm it will stand,
To 'live' with Thee e're long.

O 'mortal, why doth thou moan,
Doth not thou know God is life and love?
O 'mortal cry not alone,
Seek the Savior's gentle love.

Keep Me in Water's Still

Dear Lord, softly watch or'e my sleep,
And guide my steps each day.
Forever, holy, help me keep,
My thoughts with you today.

Keep my tongue from evil words,
And keep my hand in water's still.
Give me strength, unbroken swords,
Teach me always Thine Will.

Let not me e're rebel 'gainst Thee,
Nor let me go my way.
Keeping Christ within,
In His name, I pray.

Yielding All

Yielding all to Thee, Lord,
Resisting tempters' power.
Yielding all to Thee, Lord,
At every unbroken hour.

Yielding all to Thee, Lord,
Against the Tempers' fate.
Yielding all to Thee, Lord,
My love, thou must take.

Yielding all to Thee, Lord,
The hand of given fate.
Yielding all to Thee, Lord,
For thou art love and grace.

Yielding all to Thee, Lord,
And see Thee face to face.
Yielding all to Thee, Lord,
Ne're turn away from Thy grace.

Yielding all to Thee, Lord,
Thou conquered Satan's fee.

Yielding all to Thee, Lord,
Humbly I pray, to Thee.

Keep me ever safely,
in Christ Jesus every day.

Life

Silver moonbeams steaming through,
The starlit heaven's seeping true.

Nature's best is on its ways',
Happy, joyful, gladful days.

Ringing clear without harsh sounds,
Leaping onward, upward bound.

Restful, peaceful happy days,
Gladness comes with Sunlit Ray's.

Onward going 'till the end, Heaven's opened,
Homeward bend.

Someday 'The Latch,' I Unlock

Beyond, I see a little path,
That leads straight up a hill.
'Tis not a very wide path,
Yet, walk I there with will!

For I know 'tis not a lonely path,
Tho' the path be it straight.
For on the other side, I know,
'Tis a shining golden gate.

Someday the latch I shall unlock,
For the key I hold so dear.
Come's from Faith, I walked up on,
When once I held all fear.

No longer fear 'tis with me,
For a light t'was found within.
The key is mine and can be yours,
Let the "light of the world" win!

Beyond the little path, I know,
'Tis Glory, peace and love.
That comes from Christ, my Savior,
Who died, but lives above.

God's Hill O 'Green

In the distance t'was seen a Hill,
The color green and soft.
T'was away, the distance,
Yet, thought, I it, oft.

O' longing t'was the feeling,
For just a tiny part.
Of the Hill a' distance,
In my aching heart.

T'was all a dream to watch it,
For life t'was not my own.
And Yet 'oft times I wondered,
Lasting, should be home!

I many miles had traveled,
Toward that Hill beyond.
The longing to come near it,
In my heart b' came fond.

T'was always in the distance,
T'was something lacking, true!

And yet my longing greater,
As each prayer deeper grew.

How, ever, could I reach it?
That beauty and that rest.
And yet, I strived to gain it,
The way t'was taught me best.

Then one day thought came to me,
That darkness t'was all I'd seen!
And without the 'light' to walk in,
T'would ne're know, that Hill a' green.

I looked for 'light' and found it,
For, t'was about me everywhere!
And now I am a 'bit of green',
On that Hill, so fair!

I no longer find all a dream,
When 'The Hill', now seen ahead.
For all the 'bits' of the Father's green!
Who find it, ne're be dead.

Dost Thou Wonder and Seek?

Dost thou seek, seek and seek,
And carry burden's deep within the soul?
Dost thou fret, and fret and fret,
And worry where thouest go.

Dost thou wander in far off lands,
And never dost seem free?
Dost thou wonder in this life,
What is meant for thee.

Dost thou rarely find sleep,
Until 'wee' hours of the morn?
Dost thou sometimes wish,
That thou was't never born?

Dost thou find peace,
In any material thought?
Dost though find man,
The friend he really ought?

Dost not thou sometimes hate,
Those, we should really love?

Dost thou blame someone else,
And even Him above?

For all your transgressions and,
All your heaving sin?
And all the cares upon our heart,
That we have taken in?

Dost thou wonder what it is,
That we really lack?
For we know that even money,
Isn't what we ask.

It sort of keeps you wondering,
As you go from day to day.
But it's odd how we go as such,
And never think to pray!

We think praying's meant for sissy's,
And maids and ministers, too.
But did ever you stop to think my friend,
Praying's' meant for you!

It's funny when you forget yourself,
And seek the Lord above.
How all your fears are conquered,
And you're safe in the Fathers' love.

You find you have no worries,
And you find you have no cares.

For Jesus died to save you,
And He answers all your prayers.

Your burdens all are little ones,
When God takes you in His arms.
You never go on seeking then,
For others with false charms.

You know that His type of love,
Is great enough for all.
You know He never leaves you,
Nor does He makes you fall!

You know no matter what one may think,
If it's not the best in thought.
You don't have to listen Him,
For you know His love is naught.

With God your 'Friend' forever,
With God always at your side.
You know He's worth all your love,
In Him, you then abide.

You ask your wants in Jesus name,
You trust in Him above.
You know all things of material source,
Could never be worth His love!

You find deep peace and happiness,
You find your heart consoled.
You know that life without Christ,
Means nothing where you go.

And without the 'Great Comforter',
You'ld never find peace in life.
And you know that you'd give all wealth you owned,
To live away from strife.

Your heart is now opened,
And your joy with God, above.
The only one true friend you have,
Your only one True love.

Alone I Cannot Stand

My God, how wonderful thou art!
For thou has't lowered Thyself for men.
Thou gave us Christ, Thy Son so pure,
Now, cleansed we are from sin!

Alone, Thou knowest, we cannot stand,
For weak we be inside.
Alone to falter all that's great,
And caught in worldly tide.

Alone, weak and sinful and torn,
Alone, we'd die of shame.
But, God, Thou gave us life and love,
Need only believe upon Thy name.

My God, how wonderful thou art!
"My fortress and my rock."
Keep my faith e're strong in Thee,
Let not Thy precious name mock.

In Thee 'tis consolation and peace,
In Thee we're saved and free.
In Thee 'tis everlasting life,
Perfect peace in Eternity.

Thou Art My Rock!

My God, I place my trust in Thee,
For thou hasn't dealt with me in love.
Thou art my fortress and my rock,
My strength comes from Thee, above.

Thou has't guided me and led me,
Thou has't given life to me and fed me.
Let me ever be Thy servant,
And meet with Thee in Eternity.

Let me ever do Thine will,
Let the cross I bare.
Ne're seem great, ne're let me fail,
To see Thy Son so fair.

Give to me Thy understanding,
In matter's great or small.
Let me always come to Thee,
Ne're ever let me fall.

Pick up my weakness, make me strong,
And live my life for Thee.
Oh Lord, Thou ar't my every strength,
Forever, my Keeper, be.

To Thee To Bind

O' withering soul, O' lasting peace,
O' aching heart, giver inner lease.

O' God let my burdens ne're seem great,
And give me strength, beyond man's fate.

Ne'er let my fear be blurting, bold,
On the O' Lord conserve a' hold.

Ne'er fear the evil clutching hand,
Forever hear the peaceful band.

O' God take a' hold, and let me cling,
To Thee, my praises onward sing.

Ne're take the 'light' from my soul,
And let thy peace come be my goal.

O' God let not me be unkind,
Forever in Christ, let me bind.

Victory!!!

Crucify Him, Crucify Him,
Harshly 'they' spoke.
Crucify Him, Crucify Him,
None of gentle folk.

'They' crucified my Lord and Savior,
But Glory of life is nigh.
Christ paid for all we sinners,
In Victory now, stand by!

Impair'd Let Me Stand

Manifest Thyself in me,
Impair'd let me stand.
Ne're let me be in bondage, Lord,
To any human band.

Manifest Thyself in me,
Incumbent let me be.
To Christ Thy Son and Savior,
Who died on Calvary.

Manifest Thyself in me,
With fervency I pray.
No longer lost, forever thine,
Let not me ever stray.

Unshattered Door

O' lasting Love, my spirit rests,
Eternally upon 'Thy Breasts'.

Locking Arms around me, best,
Clinging to the Fathers' nest.

Kindness ne're as this before,
Glimpses of Unshattered Door.

O' God thou art pure in rest,
Thy wrath is great, Thy mercies best.

The Undying Sail

Oh lift my soul to Thee, O' God,
And lift my heart from stain.
Father, lock they hand in mine,
No filtering clouds, nor rain.

O' lift my innermost being high,
My God help me not fail!
Keep Thy spirit ever high,
My ship a glowing sail.

Let not the swift waters rail,
Lest I should sink, oh God!
Forever straightly help me sail,
Ne're taste the swift cruel rod.

O' God, that cross thou givest to me,
Ne're let me stray from Thee.
Keeping Christ my lasting light,
Forever and ever, Eternity.

Be Like Your Father Which Is In Heaven

Be Ye mortal...Convictions are dreams,
Be Ye immortal...'Tis God.

Be Ye of hate...'Tis mortal man,
Be Ye love...'Tis God.

Be Ye in bondage...'Tis mortal man,
Be Ye infinite...'Tis God.

God is love, Truth and of pure mind,
Mortal is weak...and blind.

Be Ye as God...sublime.

Jesus Savior Devine

My Savior loves me, I know, I know,
My Savior keeps love a glow, a glow.

My Savior helps me each day and night,
My Savior is the Son of light.

Savior I love Thee dearly,
Savior I see Thee clearly.

Savior Devine, thou art mine,
My Savior love's me so, Jesus Savior Devine.

Jesus the Shepherd of lost sheep,
Jesus is love and pure and sweet.

Jesus my Savior, I am thine,
Jesus my Savior, love sublime.

Keep me forever on hand or sea,
Keep me forever safe with Thee.

Thou art the Savior, God gave me,
My Savior, O' blessing art Thee.

~Jesus Savior Devine~

Jesus is gentle, sweet and kin,
Savior, let not me stray behind.

Guiding each footstep that I take,
Jesus, my Lord and mate.

Sweet gentle lover, keep me pure,
Sweet loving Jesus, thou art sure.

Guide all my waking hours Lord,
Ne're tasting the fate of discord.

~Jesus Savior Devine~

Keep my love a shining light,
Ne're let me ever out of sight.

Sweet loving Jesus take my soul,
Keeping me always under control.

Ne're ever let me stray away,
Keeping me safe with Thee, this day.

Let not me fall when ruff winds blow,
Keeping always my light aglow.

~Jesus Savior Devine~

My God and I

I walk with Him, my God,
He headed me to Him, oh high.
Together we found perfect peace,
Alone, my God and I.

My God and I we are alone,
But, my heart is not sad.
He helps me conquer all my fears,
Walking straightly makes me glad.

Walking alone, my God and I,
He guides me through life's strays.
But I am not sad because we're alone,
For in Christ I'm safe, all my days.

My God and I, we walk alone,
But happy I am with He.
God gives me strength and all my courage,
And with Him, I'll someday be.

The Angels of the Lord are near,
To help when we are in fear.

And with God here ever more,
He will dry my every tear.

God is great and all powerful,
God is love, you know.
God is perfect and supreme,
And to Him, I'll someday go.

Give God Your Trust!

Sometimes Lord, man is cruel,
But little does he know.
When without the Savior,
In Hell he's sure to go.

O' Lord let man realize,
The unknown stricken fate.
And Yet thou dids't send them,
The Savior, at the gate.

Thou dids't give them love, Lord,
But, man cannot see.
Thou dids't release all sin, Lord,
When trusting er'e in Thee.

O' why is man so Blind, Lord?
And, why is man so cruel?
When thou dids't give Him all, Lord,
The Son, The Golden rule.

Oh man look not away from God,
And look not down on men.

Give yourself to Christ, friend,
Released from hateful sin!

Why go on so blindly,
And why Ye always cry?
Put your trust in God, man,
Don't let the Year's slip by!

Now's the time, repent man!
Let Jesus know your sins.
Put your trust in God, man,
Eternal Life to win!

Jesus, The "Moss" Within My Being!

T'was moss I gathered on the way,
Some good, some soft, some old.
And yet each clump of hidden green,
Felt clean, and seemed pure gold.

I ran my fingers through it,
For t'was smooth and clean to feel.
T'was as a velvet warmeth,
For, I thought that it was real.

I gathered moss from hill and dale,
Along the roadway wide.
And found the 'Hidden Treasure',
About my every side.

The 'light' in darkness lingered,
And peace t'was known from core.
And much the moss that gathered,
T'was never 'felt' before.

Now grown within my person,
Apart from me ne're roam.

My earthly dreams had vanished,
My spiritual thought flown 'Home'.

The moss that I have gathered,
Is proven good and green.
For God has planted happiness, in,
That 'moss' within my being.

Did You?

Have you seen a dying soul,
Whithered torn and lost?
Did you want to save him,
At any hidden cost?

Did you long to comfort him,
And give him love and peace?
Did you know to tell him,
That sin in Christ release?

Did you hold him tightly,
And turn his tear to gold?
Or did you turn your shoulder,
And speak to him cold?

Did you find your eyes wet,
When watched him suffer there?
Did you speak to God of him,
In a silent prayer?

Did you offer shelter,
To this soul, t'was in despair?

Did you help him see our Lord,
His soul in sweet repair?

Oh, my friend if good Ye do,
With Christ, your very soul.
'Twill know the greatest treasure,
Eternal peace, the goal.

Fervent Lease!

My God, though has't redeemed me,
With Thy loving grace!
My God, how perfect thou art!
My God, at last I see Thy precious face!

My God, with Thee to never part!
Thou has't shown Thy light upon my humbled
being.
Thou has't lifted my life from darkened clay,
Thou has't given Christ, Thy Son, so keen.

With Thee in fervent prayer, I pray.

A' las, now, freed from heavy drought!
A' las, 'tis peace and life ahead!
My soul away from worldy places caught,
With Thee 'tis peace found upon my bed.

My God, my soul 'tis yours, I'm sure!
My God, Thou art my strength and peace,
My God, Thou are always pure,
In Thee I take on fervent lease.

Shepherd Be My Master

Ne're let my burdens e're seem great,
Ne're let my heart forget.
Keep me ever grateful, Lord,
O' the road of No regret.

For thou are everlasting, Lord,
No human hand can feel.
The love thou has't for all mankind,
Is true and lasting...real.

Let not me cast aside, O' Lord,
Ne're blindly let me see.
The works, the cross, the suffering,
Thou has't shed for me.

Let ne're a day go by, Lord,
Should I forget to pray.
Help me to remember, Lord,
Eternal love today.

Let each blessing thou givest,
Ne're be forgotten Lord.

Let the cross I carry,
Ne're be a broken sword.

Count me as a sheep, O' Lord,
Humbly I pray.
Shepherd be my Master,
From the ne're let me stray.

Understanding

To give with understanding,
Always goes two ways.
To give that understanding,
Makes peace for future days.

Lean a little this way,
Don't keep your thoughts within.
You may be surprised to learn,
Understanding is not a sin!

So, let's learn to understand,
Not just give out a command.
Be Ye willing, go half way,
For now and future days.

Heavenly Peace

Oh Father, I have caused Thee sorrow,
And much grief and pain.
Father, I have made Thee sad,
My heart was sin, scarlet stained.

Thou has't lifted my soul to Thee,
I sing praises to Thy name.
I glory from my very heart,
And walk this road, no longer lame.

The flower of thine heart I've found,
I pluck it with all care.
Thou gave to me Thy precious Son,
No longer now to fear.

Thy "Gentle Branch of Life," thou givest,
The lamb of God I see.
Father, Thy gracious hand leads forward,
With Christ in eternity.

Peace, joy, love, pure rest,
No gloom, nor unslept years.

For thou has't given me the 'light',
And took away my tears.

You made this road sacred to trod,
And the path narrow and straight.
Thou led me softly to thine arms',
And waite smiling at heaven's gate.

I'm happy to be thine, oh God,
For the worldly works cannot compare.
To all the peace, love and joy,
With Thee, Thy Son and loved ones to share.

The longing of Thy heavenly home,
In that "mansion with many room's."
And the place that Christ prepared for me,
I want with all to know no gloom.

Dear God, keep guiding me along,
This path the "straight and narrow."
To see Thy blissful "home," beyond,
With loving Christians on the marrow.

Brightly Did It Flame

The smoldering bit of ember lay,
Beneath the fallen coals.
The tiny little bit of spark,
T'was seeking greater goals.

T'was weight upon the bit of ember,
And nearly died away.
But a soft gentle breeze from far,
Sprung up the flame that day.

Beneath the coals the spark sprung up,
And brightly did it flame.
T'was like a golden rainbow,
No longer torn or lame.

High it reached above the earth,
The flame a glorious blaze.
Pointing straight to God, that flame,
That once was in a haze.

Eternity If Not A Dream!

Believe in me, oh my children,
I am the light, the way.
Believe in all I bring forth to Thee,
Only to God do you pray.

Ask in my name for you shall receive,
The gift of live I give.
Forget about the material source,
He who doe's in me he lives.

Believe in me and Ye shall have truth,
Love come's with abundant flow.
Believe in me and life Ye shall have,
Never from you will I go.

Trust in me for I love you,
My love is strong and supreme.
Believe in me, oh my children,
"Eternity is not a dream!"

I gave you my body and my blood,
To clear you from your sins.

It's your love I ask in return for this,
Pray now, it's the time to begin.

Turn your hearts over to me,
Let me guide you on your way.
Come to me, oh my children,
To the Blessed Father pray.

Believe in me, oh my children,
I love you all, everyone.
Believe in me, oh, my children,
I am the Father's Son.

I am the "Christ who died to save you."
I am the "Christ who made you free."
"Believe in me, oh my children,
And find peace in eternity."

Take Me O' God

Lord, take my hand and guide my way,
And lead me places strong.
Forever shed Thy grace on me,
Ne'er let me do no wrong.

Take me in thine arms and love me,
Keep the Son e're nigh.
Let not me ever suffer death,
Ne'er foolishly e're cry.

Lord, take my soul and make it pure,
And cleanse my heart from sin.
Hold thine hand upon my head,
And let the "sun" come in.

Ne're let me go about in blindness,
Keep my soul er'e pure.
Let me always do thine will,
The evil force er'e pure.

Nev'r let me in lameness walk,
Ner'e foreign soil know.
Keep my soul above with Thee,
My narrow path aglow.

Listen Sinning 'Churchman'

Listen Sinning 'Churchman',
That the spirit may be saved.
Listen Sinning 'Churchman',
To the Savior Christ God gave.

Let not your sins dwell with you,
Let not your fear take hold.
Listen to our Savior,
His wealth is more than gold.

Listen Sinning 'Churchman',
And receive eternal peace.
Listen to our Savior,
Our sins in him release.

Listen all ye 'Churchman',
Become wholesome day by day.
Listen Sinning 'Churchman',
In Jesus name ye pray.

Drink not the cup unworthily,
For it's certain death to you.

Listen Sinning 'Churchman',
Find peace beyond the blue.

It is God who give us courage and strength,
It is He who love us all.
It is God we seek for comfort,
When paths are near the fall.

It is God who knows troubled minds,
It is God who guides us straight.
It is He who sees us through our ways,
It is God our great, who waites'.

He is always near for comfort,
For He ner'e leaves our side.
If you are without wisdom,
Go to Him, abide!

He will ease your heart from pain,
For He understands us well.
Go to Him with heavy load,
Release it, He wants for you to tell.

'Tis God We Seek

Let not they be your worries,
For 'tis you they do not care.
Let not they disturb you,
Nor take away your share.

Of trust and wisdom of our lord,
Who watches us on high.
For 'tis God of whom we seek,
To guide our pathways nigh.

'Tis He who knows our wisdom,
And answers every prayer.

So, seek the Lord God so Great,
And give Him anguish none.
Keep your mind with only Him,
And find at end, peace is won.

Peace

Air'e Ye go, air'e Ye be.

Blinding eyes, never hearing.

Fateless wonder, boundless glow.

Seeking on, found misery.

Clinching fists, tightly set,

Yearning what, knowing not.

Forgetting "man" that "He" begot.

Always taxing, ne'er relaxing

Thinking only of thine self.

Open hearts to music high.

Finding Christ here, there, nigh!

Find Peace in Eternity

Why dost thou weep, O' little friend?
There's beauty all around.
Art thou friendless, my little friend?
Wake up from Satans' bound!

Dost thou love death, or dost thou want life?
My little friend look not away.
Trusting your heart to God the Father,
In Jesus name do pray.

Look not for sorrow, my little friend,
Look not for gloom everywhere!
Place all your trust in God the Son,
Finding beauty and love with Him there.

Speak with my God, O' little friend,
He helped once when as you.
He made my tears glow as the sun.
Ask Him, he'll help you too!

Place all your trust in Him, little friend,
Feat not! For He loves you all.

Open your heart, let Him come in,
Answer my Saviors call!

He died on the cross, my little friend,
For folks such as you and I.
He bled and suffered for our sins,
That we may never die!

Oh come now! My little friend,
Let Jesus dry your tears.
Give Him your heart today, my friend,
Vanished and gone are all fears.

Walking the long, straight narrow path,
Leading beyond all sea.
Lift up your head to God, my friend,
Find peace now and in Eternity.

One Mind in Christ

My friends and I are of one mind,
'Tis proven O'er and O'er.
And when I meet another kind,
'Tis hard to reach the core.

For I speak of another world,
And they do not understand.
They think the world I speak of,
Is a strange and unknown land.

And yet, they, too, can have it,
If they'd place my God above.
Their earthly wild possessions,
They cling to and they love.

We then could see eye to eye,
Walk hand in hand together.
Fight all storms and evil cry,
In any kind of weather.

The "Sun" would brightly shine above,
The earth then be so small.

T' would know God's pure and lasting love,
For man both great and small.

But, my friends and I are of one mind,
My enemies of another.
'Tis hard to mix with their kind,
So t' will fellowship with my brother.

The Lord of My Soul

The dripping of blood upon a snow white gown,
The blood beneath a thorn pierced crown.

The shame He bore from sin and disgrace,
My 'Lord' died to prove His grace.

.

He bore all wickedness we implanted,
He bore all grief we chanted.

Again and again men listen not,
To the Son, God begot.

O' lift up thine face and let the tears roll,
Suffer the Cross, and suffer the toll.

Bend humbly at the Saviors feet,
Repent now, suffer not defeat.

O' Father let Thy will approach,
Goodness and mercy thou dost coach.

Give unto me Thy wisdom and love,
Teach me to love as a 'turtle dove'.

Come humbly to Thy Godly gate,
To find Thee, now, my gentle mate.

Let not the shame He bore for all,
Be forsaken on misguided call.

Let all come with humbleness,
And know the Savior's heavenliness.

Dear Father, let us follow straight,
Thy narrow path heading to Thy gate.

Where Christ will hold the 'sheep' so dear,
And know no woe, nor sorrow and fear.

Help us go Thy way, O' Lord,
The hand of God ties the cord.

God Be With You, 'Till We Meet Eternally

God be with you, 'till we meet again,
For wishing this with you is more than gold.
Heaven is not weighted in material gain,
Heaven's the like above untold.

God be with you 'till we meet again,
For with God, you never have a fear.
God so great, so kind and good,
With God, vanished are the tears.

God be with you 'till we meet again,
God never leaves your side.
God is gracious and forgives sins,
These troubles with you in Him confide.

So, God be with you 'till we meet again,
His love is Supreme, good and true.
God be with you 'till we meet again,
Beyond the silvery blue.

The Voice Where Air'e I Go

Who art thou calling me?
'Tis a voice I do not know.
A haunting straining echo,
This voice where air'e I go.

What does thou want of me?
This voice I do not know.
'Tis a haunting, haunting echo,
This voice, where air'e I go.

T'was fear that kept my answer,
Deep within my heart.
T'was fear that kept my Savior,
And me these Years apart.

T'was fear that kept Christ hidden,
From my cluttered mind.
T'was fear that kept my Lord and King,
Those many years, behind.

At last I reached a climax,
And needed desperately.

To cleanse my soul in whiteness,
My sins all set free.

But, how this should happen, the way,
I did not know.
Then one day I listened,
For "The voice where air'e' I go."

I listened close, as it grew faint,
In calling all these years.
But, it softly spoke to me, and,
Cleansed my heart from fears.

Each day it grew louder,
And now I understood.
T'was ever, ever calling me,
Come, under heavens' hood.

'Tis bliss to know God called me,
To join the humble band.
These tens' O' thousands soldiers,
Who follow God's command.

He spoke of Christ "The Savior,"
Who opened life for me.
He wants me as a branch on,
The Blessed family tree.

That voice, no longer a stranger's, for,
I know that voice, now, well.
Just listen all ye people,
And, it too you can tell.

Of the Christ who died to save you,
Of the Christ who knows you well.
Listen all you people I know,
I know, well.

Let not fear over take you,
On this road, 'tis just a day.
Give your heart to Jesus,
Release your sins and pray.

He's a loving Savior, cause,
He died that all may live.
Beyond the Blue Horizon,
His Life for all did give.

God So Loved The World

Jesus died to save us,
From this world of sin.
God so loved the world,
Through Jesus He lets us in.

On His right He sits, Heaven,
There, with God he is.
Practice and do the Ten Commandments,
By doing so we become His.

Yes, God so loved the world,
For He gave us Jesus His Son.
That "Who so-ever believeth in Him,"
Shall have life, and peace is won.

The Steadfast Ship

O' ship a' sailing ov'r the waves,
On ocean wide and green.
This silver coat of shiniest steel,
That I had ever seen.

The waves O' ruff but sails not torn,
And anchor strung on side.
This ship a' sailing ov'r the waves,
Found peace above the wide.

The ship strong and steadfast stood,
The sails looked straight to God.
Eternal sail t'was its' goal,
The golden sea to shod.

The ship stood fast in heavy storms,
That beat against the bow.
Ne're ever did it change its' course,
Ne're did it sink below.

Eternal ages t'was reward,
For the ship that look to God.
The battle won and Christ now had,
No sting of wrath and rod.

My Voice In Music Rings

You ask me why, I speak of Christ my King?
I cannot lie, Christ makes me laugh and sing.

He turned the gloom, to sun instead of rain,
He is my groom, I love Him not in vain.

Christ saved my soul, and I no longer cry,
He made my life pure, no longer now defy.

He deals with love, to all who ask of Him,
And, from above, He waites, t'will win.

You ask me why, I love my Lord and King?
You ask me why, my voice in music rings?

You ask me why, no longer tears fall nigh?
And I will tell, for you and me he died!

He gave His life, to save my soul from doom,
He placed smiles, in my lonely room.

He drove away, all cares, doubts and tears,
In Christ, I have no fears.

Let Me Prove Myself!

Oh Father thou hast proved to me,
In many simple ways.
That, thou has't loved me for now,
And eternal days.

Thou has't made me strong in Thee,
Thy peace thou has't given me.
Father, thou has't shown me favor,
With Christ, in eternity.

Thou has't given Thy only Son,
Thou has't set us free.
Father, thou has't given all,
To prove Thy love for me.

I long to see Thy blessed home,
I long with Christ to be.
With all Thy glorious Christian folk,
In peaceful eternity.

Oh, Father, this short span of material life,
Let me do Thy will.

Help others find our loving Christ,
Who died on Calvary's Hill.

Let us all take up our cross,
No longer lost sheep be.
Dear Father, thou has't given all,
Now let me give to Thee.

My Lord Is Merciful

The Lord is merciful and slow to anger,
He forgives your blackened soul.
Whips the scares and stains of sins,
And leads you places straight to go.

He guides each footstep for those who ask,
And makes your daily tasks a pleasure.
He gives you love and holy grace,
He left you with life's treasure.

All this on earth is His, you know,
You came with nothing and return the same.
Keep in mind the Son, God gave,
Go 'bout not blindly, hopelessly, lame.

Let your heart not be stubborn,
Let the 'sun' creep through.
God has chosen all to come,
In the hand beyond the blue.

He sent the Shepherd to guide lost sheep,
We are all sheep, you know.

The Shepherd is the Christ our King,
He leads you safely, the path to go.

It's narrow, straight, rugged and long,
The cross we take up now.
We follow in the way of light,
At times er' with sweated brow.

We learn that all, is not enough,
To prove we are worthy of Him.
For "God so loved the world," you know,
N' gave Jesus to free us of sin.

The earthly gains are destructions and hell,
When we place them before our God.
Take up, now, the cross O' man,
Follow the light, abroad.

God is Near, There is No Fear

Thou knowest all the evil, Lord,
Implanted in my heart.
Thou knowest all the terror, Lord,
Taken on my part.

Thou knowest when I forsake Thee, Lord,
Thou knowest the material gain.
Could never fully capture me,
For man is driven rain.

Thou knowest when I stray from Thee,
Thou knowest deepest thoughts.
Thou knowest, Lord, I need Thee always,
When in Satan's hand I'm caught.

Thou comest at that hour, Lord,
Thou drivest away those fears.
Thou makest the rain glow like the sun,
When taking away my hidden tears.

Thou knowest that I love Thee,
Even in that darkest hour.
Thou knowest fully I re-gain Thee Lord,
In fighting Satans' wicked power.

Ner'e Let Me Go, O' Lord!

Oh God, I give my soul to Thee,
  And clinging to thine hand.
  Releasing Satans' power,
  The stricken evil band.

I give my heart to Thee, O' Lord,
  And give my humbled self.
  A meager little handful,
  A small unknown elf.

I am, but one small man, O' God,
  In this world of many men.
But thou has't saved my soul from wrath,
  And released my heart from sin.

Take my humbled being, Lord,
  Ner'e let me taste death's fate.
  Ner'e let me ever falter,
  Nor taste the 'Hand of Hate'!

I beg Thee, Lord, to take me,
  In the land without an end.

Placing trust with Thee, Lord,
And the One thou d' send.

Take me in thine arms, Lord,
Hold me close to Thee.
Ner'e let me out of sight, Father,
Take me in eternity.

Little Children

Little children do not fear,
The good Lord, God, is ever near.

Praise Him, keep Him, love Him all,
He will guide you, so paths won't fall.

Honor His memory in all your thoughts,
Keep Him holy has been taught.

Let Him lead you on your way,
To the bright land, far someday.

'Tis Visible

I lay and watch the clouds pass by,
With interest I glance above.
And simple are the figures made,
But, scenes I truly love.

For, I know that all is good and clean,
And pure and bright and right.
For, God mad all this visible,
To my faulty sight.

'Tis a figure of an old kind face,
And one of flower or tree.
Look! Here's one of Christ, my Savior,
Who died that I might see!

The clouds go by, and I watch with hope,
And faith comes from within.
For Christ has saved me fully,
From wrath and evil, sin.

I lay and watch the clouds go by,
And know 'tis not a dream.
For, God has planted all, 'tis good,
For wanting souls, a gleam!

My Prayer

Dear God, 'tis not the good in Thee,
That, speak the evil, 'tis the evil in me.

'Tis not words of good, hat comes forth from me.
But, 'tis the good from Thee.

Oh my precious Father.
Put Thy good in me.
Help me watch the evil,
Brought forth from me.

Help me always keep in contact with Thee,
Dear God
Keep me safe each day, from evil works,
Brought forth from evil rod.

In Jesus, Thy beloved Son,
I ask and pray,
To guide me safely,
All the way.

Amen.

Beneath The Unknown Voices Cry!

Trampled branch of fallen tree,
And treaded down beneath the sea.

Torn and lost, and withered sigh,
Beneath the unknown voices cry!

O' broken branch from fallen grace,
O' never knowing loving face.

And bedded down beneath wild force,
Ner'e knowing glory, 'tis such remorse.

O' pick Thy branch to lands ahead!
And let Thy dusty pathway shed.

All film and darkened evil clay,
No longer 'neath the water lay.

O' pick Thyself above the shod!
And find eternal peace with God.

Ner'e tarry long, the shaded path,
O' gather up! And know not wrath!

Let that branch of fallen life,
O' walk in 'light', away from strife.

Ner'r gather stoney seed nor foam,
Nor let thy self, unworthy roam.

O' broken branch, come mend Thy ways,
Finding peace, and gladdened days.

Ner'e let Thy gentle branch be lost,
Tinging life, Christ, payed the cost!

Spiritually Linger

Let me do my duty, Lord,
To Thee in every way.
Let me always linger,
In spiritual thought, today.

Caution me and guide me,
When in distress, I stand.
Nor dubious let me wonder,
Amid the frozen land.

Cast Thy 'Light' upon me,
Visible to my eye.
Ner'e let me go 'bout blindly,
Abash, nor foolishly sigh.

Restrain my tongue from evil,
Give strength to amend my way.
Let me do my duty, Lord,
To Thee, I humbly pray.

Is Man Perfect? No!

Man is so imperfect,
For one day he seems above.
The nexed day he can be so hasty,
And never think of love.

Man can go on yearning,
And never find the way.
Man can go on being,
Sinful, every day.

Man can go on dreaming,
And find only artificial songs.
But man forever without God,
Is up against the 'throngs'.

Man without Christ the Savior,
Is lost, beyond repair.
Man without God to lead Him,
Is in utter, wild despair.

Man go'est on so blindly,
When he thinks only of man.
But, man with The Savior,
Is safe in God's holy hand.

Your Golden Dreams

I never go by fashions,
I never go by dates.
I never go by etiquette,
I never go by mates.

I never go by sayings,
I never go by songs.
I never go by newspapers,
Too often they are wrong.

I never go by people,
Who claim to know it all.
For often times when listening them,
I come nearer the hateful fall.

The "Book" I put my nose in,
And answers found, there, sure.
Are never one's to laugh at,
Never one's to sneer.

One's true self is discovered,
The true life is supreme.

When going by the Bible,
You find life is not a dream.

My hear is full with richness,
For I know that I am saved.
Christ died to save we sinners,
His life a 'ransom' gave.

God is ever calling friends,
Take heed now to His call.
It isn't only a few God wants,
'Tis you and me and all.

His love is great, beyond all seas,
His glory is of grace.
God's waiting 'home' for you and me,
With love upon His face.

His arms are stretched around us,
He's calling all to come.
Home, beyond the blue vast skies,
With Jesus, His beloved Son.

Open your hearts and let Christ in,
Give Christ your hearts own key.
Let Him open that little door,
Come in forever in eternity.

He loves you all, every one,
He calls you all this day.
He wants for you to know true life,
Release your heart in God do pray.

Let Him lead each footstep,
That you take upon this road.
Let Him always guide you,
Yourself with God abode.

Make Christ your lasting dwelling place,
He has an endless home.
God the Father gave His Son,
For man to have a lasting dome.

He proves to be your own true friend,
He never lets you down.
He loves you all with depth and purity,
He died with a thorn pierced crown.

What more could he do to prove His love?
For he gave His very life.
Only need to believe this true,
In return receive eternal life.

Open your hearts and let Him enter,
Follow the Lord God high.
Give yourself to Christ today!!
Never in damnation die.

No Longer Discontentment

One can be so weary,
If with troubled mind.
Nothing can be pleasing,
No one sweet or kind.

Why is it so for some,
That life dost seem this way?
For others things are pleasant,
Happy thoughts to help their way.

With some it's just discontentment,
The reason not fully known.
As we know the rights, and, know the wrongs,
That from one's heart love grown.

We do wish and want contentment,
And not a troubled heart.
To lead us to that peaceful place,
When, from this world depart.

The things I dream of in my mind,
Of the great world beyond.

Are happy peaceful thoughts,
Far from material bond.

And yet at times I wondered,
For they spoke to me of hell.
And I know my soul is blackened,
'Cause Satan's sure to tell!

I've looked all around me,
And know the world's a 'sight'.
And yet, alone, can't help myself,
Find that happy 'light'.

So many time t'was near me,
And yet I couldn't see.
Many times I tarred, and,
Alone, I cried to Thee.

Then fervently I knelt in prayer,
And peace then appeared.
Thou taught me love and lasting life,
My heart no longer speared.

Then Christ was put before me,
And all that he had done.
Died and suffered for my sins,
And taught me things to shun.

I let Him come in my heart,
And life there now exist.
No longer going blind about,
His road I not resist.

When?

When things don't go your way,
God is there.

When in times of grief and pain,
God is there.

When the blood stained cross Jesus bore, seems far
away, God is there.

When all the misery life deals out, you have known,
God is there.

At these times, listen close, 'cause,
God is here.

It's easy to listen God calls from nigh and near,
God is here.

Burden's all are loosened from beneath, 'cause,
God is here.

Pray, release all sorrow felt within,
God is here.

Life of peace, joy and love freely come, 'cause,
God is near.

Eternal rest is at hand when man doe's God's will,
Listen, listen close my friend,

God is ever here.

The Beauty of Light

Some find beauty in books,
Some find endless rides and nook.

But in quiet things beauty for me abounds,
They are things with simple sounds.

Just a nod from an understanding form,
One glance at flower and tree,
Something God had made for me.

Beauty isn't, to me, artificial song,
But the song which lingers year and year along.

Some find beauty in a building tall and china doll,
But without God, man could make nothing,
Even small.

'Tis beauty in a blade of grass,
For 'tis beauty in the shades of green amass.

'Tis beauty in animal great or small,
For only God can make such beauty for all.

Look at the moon, the stars and the sky,
Only God can make such beauty a' high.

'Tis such beauty all around to find,
Man could find greater beauty.
If choosing so in time,
For God gave a 'light', greater than mankind.

He gave us the beauty of Christ, His Son,
In Him the greatest beauty
And victory of all beauty won!

My Precious Love

I found a precious love,
And love Him deeply and true.
For my precious love,
Keeps me from feeling blue.

I trust my precious love,
And find Him pure and sweet.
My precious love above mankind,
Ner'r the elite.

He's gentle, soft and tender,
And deals with kindness every day.
He never leaves me fretful,
Nor along to decay.

He helps me carry all burdens,
My best along the way.
He wipes my tears,
Fall that may.

My precious love is thoughtful,
He never leaves me alone.

He never causes fearfulness,
Nor leaves me to groan.

He always is beside me,
Gives strength for every task.
Nor does he ever forsake me,
But gives me more than I ask.

He treats me with all kindness,
He loves me and makes me glad.
He never causes me to be fearful,
And lifts me when I'm sad.

He gives me strength and courage,
And all my daily bread.
He never lets me linger,
In places that men dread.

He points out all the wonders,
Of beauty in every form.
He places smiles about me,
His face of pureness adorn.

My precious love is Jesus,
The 'Son God gave' to all.
The world all listen to Him,
Hear His gentle call.

Always "Keep" My Daily Being

When away I stray, oh Lord,
Emotions of self-pity forth they come.

Oh Father, help me keep my heart with Thee,
Let me find, above, they home.

Lord, keep my thoughts pure,
And my soul clean.

Keep my safe, never dwell in lands unseen,
Oh God, Thou art my daily being.

Apostle Paul

Saul threatening and slaughtering the
disciples of the Lord.

Desired a letter from the high priest to
destroy those of the Word!

And as he journeyed near Damascus to
destroy there, the word.

A light came from heavens, it was the Lord.

Saul fell to the earth and a voice to Him said,
why persecutest thou me, Saul?

For Thee I have bled!

And Saul trembling and astonished, said Lord,
what wilt thou me do?

"Arise!" go to the city and thou shalt learn
there what to do!

And, the men which journeyed with him stand there
awed!

For they thought that this Jesus was
buried and dead!

Saul rose from the earth and opened his eyes and
looked to the heavens but could not see the skies!

The men led him away, for he saw no man, and
brought him to Damascus, led him by hand!

And there Ananias, the disciple of the Lord, put his
hand on Saul by the word of the Lord!

His sight all restored with the Holy Ghost, now
filled.

This chosen vessel of God now for Christ,
he'd been killed!

Then to the Synagogues he preached Jesus is Lord,
believe and baptized, Jesus is The Word.

But all that heard him were amazed and said it is not this be who destroyed many, for This One, now dead?

But Paul increased in strength and confounded the Jews are with the news, this the Christ who died for us all!

The Jews became angry and planned to kill Saul, but this plot he knew and escaped by the wall.

What love for this Master? Yet! What love from a King! Could Paul ask more?

Nay, Christ's everything.

Thou Art "The Adored"

My God, I place my trust in Thee,
For thou art pure in heart.
Thou led me away from worldly gain,
And gave me a rightful start.

Thou has't set a goal to reach,
That alone I could not attain.
For I need Thy strength always Lord,
Eternal peace my gain.

Thy Heavens' of bliss and longing,
And the star from earth not seen.
Oh so few with find it Father,
This place I've never been.

Give grace and mercy to us all,
Oh God, keep me under Thy Throne.
Let me always see the love,
That Christ Thy Son has't shown.

Never let me do my will,
But only thine, my Lord.
Let me always prove to Thee,
Thou art the one adored.

A Command To One's Self

Let nothing ever take away,
The things you've fought for till this day.

Let no one every make you regret,
Remember Christ, lest you forget.

The suffering, toil and endless tasks,
You looked to God, "mercy you asked."

Him above to help you find,
The peace you needed, no withered grind.

Look not away from Christ, nor regret,
Look not away, lest you forget.

Fulfillment

It seemed as though I'd never see the sun on high!

When my sunken dreams found, shattered, gone.

And then I looked above the clouds,
and saw the sun a brilliant glow.

Shinning bright, above the earth,
At last clouds rolled past.

Now dreams no longer,
For they aside were cast.

And truth came forth as brightly as the sun.

For Christ had filled my heart with peace when,
He, in my life began.

The Poor Rich Man!

In purple and fine linen,
The rich man was arrayed.
Selfish and greedy,
For His soul ner'e prayed.

Sickly with sores,
And begging for food.
Poor Lazarus, the beggar,
At rich man's gate stood.

Hungry for crumbs fallen,
From the rich man's table.
Dogs licking His sores,
Shewing them away unable.

But the rich man cared not,
'Bout this poor sickly man.
Who laid at His gate,
Begging food from His hand.

Then one day Lazarus died,
And angels carried Him to heaven.

With tenderest love,
To Abraham's bosom.

But the rich man died too,
And he was buried.
And in hell lifted His eyes,
To Abraham, where Lazarus was carried.

"Father Abraham," he cried,
In His torment and tears.
Send Lazarus, with water,
Oh my soul is with fears.

I am tormented with flames!
Cool my tongue from this pain.
"Father Abraham" he called,
But His calling was vain.

Then Abraham spoke, saying,
"Son remember in life.
Thou receivedst good things,
Lazarus, the evil," the strife!

But now he is comforted,
And thou art tormented.

There lies a gulf between us,
Where help is prevented.

Then said the rich man,
I pray Thee Father.
Send Lazarus to earth,
That he may warn my five brothers.

Of the torment in hell,
Oh, this pain hard to be near.
Oh, send Him Father Abraham,
That they not come here!

But Abraham said unto Him,
"It is now much too late!
For they believed not the prophets,
Nor Moses, whom they hate!

Nor would they believe,
One who rose from the dead.
For Jesus already gave,
His life for their stead!

In My Heart Begin

Purge my heart with pureness,
Cleanse my clean from sin.
Keep me pure and sweet, Lord,
Let no evil in.

Give me understanding,
And knowledge bright of Thee.
Lord, oh be my master,
Thy spirit in me be.

Oh God, my Father Holy,
Look not away from me.
Let me always worship,
Thee and only Thee!

Keep me safe in travels,
Land, sea or dale.
Let Thy spirit linger,
Within my humble sail.

Oh God, sweet loving Savior,
Thou cleansed me clean of sin.
Always be my strong hold.
In my heart begin.

The Loss Too Great

My heart t' was lonely,
My friends a' few were mine.
Endless empty hours,
Boundless time.

Then Thou filled days of joy,
Gladness came with Golden rays.
Lord always keep within my being,
Praying faith fully I do today.

Not tomorrow, no longer lingers,
Of thoughts of Thee, dear Lord.
For daily does't Thou always linger,
In my deep unspoken cord.

Thy hand leads gently over me,
My feet Thy way not stay.
No longer heartaches, nor am lonely,
With Thee I bind today.

Thy light thou gaves't 'tis all I ask,
And saved now be I, Lord.
Away from Thee no longer go I,
The loss I cannot, now afford!

Forgiveness!

Oh Judas had Ye repented,
End gone to the Lord.

That day, last soul, even,
Thou'd been saved by His word.

I shudder to think that,
It could've been I!

I thank Thee, Oh Lord,
Saved by Thy blood!

No Longer 'Blind'

Once a year or two ago,
Things I thought I knew t' weren't so!

And all because no light within,
Thy heart full of sin.

I cried and looked and seeked and begged,
I cried upon my weary bed.

And no help came,
For I was lame.

"Oh God!" one night my soul cried out,
And begged for help, with loudest shout.

My soul was torn and lost,
And this I knew, but not the cost!

For doomed t' was I, sure as death,
My heart t' was pierced, and head with wreath.

Oh God, give me peace! I cried,
This I called upon my side.

And it seemed a year passed by,
My soul again to God did cry.

"Oh Father God, give me peace,
Give my shrunken soul release!"

And then knelt I alone,
And God did hear me groan.

T'was like bit O' softness and a feeling of pure bliss.
For I know that he was with me, 'cause he soothed
my restlessness.

And then I knelt fervently to pray,
And begged Him, with me, stay.

And stay he did forever more,
And gave me peace and beauty for.

Step by step he taught and led me,
Step by step he guided, fed me.

And then His Son to me came clear,
Why Christ died to forgive fears.

And this my heart once resisted,
For this was the part in life I missed.

But God heard me pray,
And gave me Christ that day.

Music Perfect

Thou art music to my soul,
God, thou art my goal.

Thou art Hope and Joy,
Thou art Hope and Joy.

Christ, thou gavest to free us all,
Joyful I answer Thy call.

He Plants Gold Dust

With Christ one has love and hope and peace,
With Christ one's soul is not torn – always release.

With Christ no gloom, but smiles abroad and far,
For Christ takes His place and puts gold dust in each
star.

With Christ all fear is gone - no tears' nor pain,
With Christ the sun shines gloriously bright, no
rain.

With Christ no shadow can befall,
With Christ eternity is meant for all.

The rapture of each heart now complete,
With Christ no struggle nor defeat.

With Christ is love forever more,
With Christ is life for all, Him adore.

With Christ within each humane heart,
Friends and loved ones never part.

Be Not A Fool!

Oh man, such fools thou art,
When from God, thou art apart.

Pick up thy pieces of broken Life,
Walk with Christ, away from strife.

Keep Him first in your heart,
Let no one keep you apart.

Believe in His gentle command,
Come oh man, take Thy stand!

Look not away this day, dear friend,
Come to Christ, Thy Life will blend.

Peace, truth and power in Him,
Come to Christ, Let Him win!

Man, Oh man, be not a fool!
Let not Satan make you a tool!

Let our Savior rule all and all,
Come, Oh friend, hear His call.

'Tis peace and bliss and happiness,
Come receive His perfect kiss.

Come to home, with God all three,
Father, Son, and Spirit - Eternity.

Joyful End

Oh my God, Thou art pure,
Blessed, Sacred, soft and sure.

Thou has't given Happiness,
In Thee there is no restlessness.

Thou has't given all for me,
Thy Son to free me, now I see.

My eyes are opened wide and clear,
In my heart there is no fear.

Oh my God how perfect thou art,
From Thee not apart, not apart.

Eternity is life - no end,
Peaceful hope, joyful end.

He Truly Cares!

I see beyond the sunset,
One glorious day ahead.
That we Christians all will witness,
Because Jesus died and bled.

One grand, beautiful reunion,
With all our loved ones there.
And this we all will witness,
Because Our Savior cares.

He died that we may not suffer,
The death of ours, and despair.
But Jesus did all this for us,
Our Savior truly cares.

In Victory He Lives

My Savior loves me, this I know,
For he died at the cross for me.
He arose again to God in glory,
And conquered all in victory.

He died at the cross that I may live,
He suffered in torment for me.
He bore the crown that I should bear,
My Savior died in victory.

Yes, my Savior truly lives,
He's now with the Father High.
Yes, my Savior truly loves,
He did all that I not die.

He tenderly watches or'e His sheep,
And the sheep are they that believe.
Yes, my Savior loves me true,
My all to Him, I receive.

Not Lost, But Saved!

A lost little lamb who strayed away,
Thirsted and hungered all the day.

Feebly from place to place it strayed,
And never once it prayed.

Torn and bruised and all at last,
All spiritual help away he did cast.

Sweated and worn and aid not seen,
For this lamb, the unforeseen.

All had forsaken this bit of life,
And slowly it would give up with the strife.

He laid at last on His side to cry,
No longer this struggle, God let me die!

And a small voice came clear to Him,
"Let me come in, come in."

Who art thou? The lamb did ask,
"Between you and I there lies a mask."

But the voice louder this time said,
"I am Jesus who suffered for all and bled."

Let me come into your heart today,
There isn't much time, do not delay.

I've waited these many years for you,
Let me come in and make you anew.

The lamb raised up from the ground he lay,
And looked straight ahead to God that day.

"Oh Father God" he cried with a sigh,
"How can you love such a worm as I?"

But the lamb was assured Christ died
for the sinners,
And gave Him His heart to become
one of the winners.

Rejoice

Let us rejoice for it's Christmas,
The time of the Saviors birth.
Let us sing praise and carols,
Beside our cozy warm hearth.

Let us be glad of salvation,
The "gift" God gave to all men.
Let us rejoice for it's Christmas,
And be glad we are free from all sin.

Could It Be?

Could it be,
That he died.
'Cause my burdened,
Heart had cried?

'Cause my soul,
Was torn, bled.
Weighted sins,
I couldn't shed?

'Cause no cloak,
For my sin.
Was ever known,
'Till he came in.

This wicked world,
Yet conquered he.
The sins of all,
On Calvary's' tree.

Yes, I know,
'Tis why he came.
My sins released,
In His precious name!

John 14: Little Sheep Of Mine

"Let not your heart be troubled,"
Jesus said to me,
"I go and prepare a place for you,
And receive you unto me."

In my Father's house are many mansions,
If it were not so, you'ld know.
That there I am, little sheep,
There ye may also go.

And whither I go ye know,
And the way ye also know.
My sheep will hear my voice,
And follow me, the way to go.

I am the way, the truth, the life,
No man cometh unto the Father but by me.
Ye should have known the Father,
If ye had known me!

Let not your heart be troubled,
My master said to me.

If ye know the Master's voice,
Then ye shall have my peace!

Avoid the storm the Thunder loudly cried,
The streaks of lightening blazed across the
darkened sky.

And, shrieking back with fear embedded deep,
I wondered "who" would come and be my Keep.

It seemed the storm would never pass away,
For, the fear was rooted deep within the clay.

And, there above the cold darkened sky,
My eyes peeled to the "Sun" on high.

I stood still a moment, but,
it seemed eternity,
And, placed the struggle,
In the Hands of Someone fair.
And, found that God had touched my heart,
Which quickly ceases all care.

For he had come,
and washed the earth bright and clean,

And even though it was just Yesterday.
He gave me Christ who,
Drove my fears away, today.

Praise God the Father

Just a prayer of praise and thanks to Thee, dear God.
Just a prayer of love and joy to Thee.

For thou has't blest us all with grace and holiness.
Thou dear Father God, brought all Happiness.

Praise, oh praise to God who loves the world.
Praise, oh praise to Thee Dear Lord of Host.

Thou art all mankind could ask, and more.
Thou art the Father of the Savior of the world.

My Thanksgiving

Lord, I thank Thee for this day of joy and peace.
I thank Thee for the sins thou did release.

I thank Thee for Thy faithfulness.
I thank Thee for Thy tenderness.

Lord I thank Thee for all blessings great and small.
But, Lord, I thank Thee for Thy Son most of all!

I thank Thee daily for the life I lead.
To be in paradise with Thee, just to believe.

That Christ is Lord.

Amen

Only One

There's only one life and one love alone,
There's only one joy and one alone.
There's only one path and one alone,
There's only One and it's Jesus.

There's only one God and one alone,
There's only one Savior and one alone.
There's only one Heaven and one alone,
And these are all my Jesus.

There's only one day and one alone,
There's only one Christ and one alone.
There's only one who died for us all,
And He is only Jesus, That's all!

Blessings

Bless us oh Lord and guide all our way.
Give us Thy strength from day to day.

Lead us in paths of righteousness.
Keep evil away, and gave us holiness.

Help us to read fervently Thy word.
That we may be used, for only Thy word.

Bless those about us and keep all secure.
For Thou only God art pure.

In Jesus Thy Son, who has saved us from sin.
I pray the oh Lord for blessings within.

Only Thou Cans't Take Away The Shadows

Dark shadows in the night,
And through the day the rain.
Dark shadows crowding close,
And fills my heart with deepest pain.

How lonely and heavy drags the endless days,
Due mostly to the storm within any soul ablaise.

Only Thee, great One of all,
Can cleanse the shadows that around me fall.

Only Thee cans't make my soul a glowing Light,
And take away the shadows day and night.

For thou, Lord, the giver of all gifts of Love,
Gave us Christ Thy Son,
That we may dwell safe with the Above.

Lord I Am Unworthy

For thee to love me so.

But in spite of all my downfalls,
Thou away from ne're go.

How much and long to see Thee.

Thou I'm unworthy to see Thy face.

Lord I thank Thee that thou saved me,
By Thy precious loving grace.

A Pleading Heart

O' Lord, keep Thy face not from me,
How long wilt thou stay away?
Keep not Thy face from me, Lord,
I no longer can a' stray.

Thou has't lead me out of 'Egypt',
Thou has't shown me grace.
Keep not love for me, Lord,
Let me see Thy face.

How I Long For Thee, My Sweet One

'Tis a sad and lonely eve,
It seems like years since Yesterday.

'Tis truly hard to believe,
That only a wee few hours
Have passed since seeing you.

Darling ask men not if I love you,
For t'would grieve my soul, and you.

Now you know that my longing,
Should not be the way it is.

Nevertheless my dearest sweetheart,
'Tis something I don't regret.

Keep My Spark A' glow

Oh sweet gentle loving Jesus,
Make me more and more like Thee.
Never, ever let me tarry,
Places, I should never see.

Guide my pathway Gentle Jesus,
Up and down the roadway wide.
Never, ever let me falter,
Keep my love a glowing pride.

Precious Jesus, gentle Savior,
Save 'that' humble room for me.
Let me always love and trust Thee,
Rest my head upon Your knee.

Keep Thy hand upon me, Jesus,
So from Thee I not astray.
Help me keep my spark a' glowing,
In eternity this day.

Victory Won

That haunting, wracking, turmoil within my being.
That haunting, sordid soul, the unforeseen!

O' t' will ner'e it set me free at peace?
T'will wreck my soul, t'won't release!

Ner'e friend nor foe to understand.
I plead to Thee, O' helping hand!

What be it, Lord? I do not know.
It follows constant, where I go.

In my every waking hour and restless sleep.
T'will it ever, be my keep?

Turn not t' whom, that, know not I.
I plead, I beg, and brokenly sigh.

O' Lord must always, this, my fate be?
Open my heart, help me see.

I need Thee Lord, I need Thee all.
O' Lord, in vain let not me call.

Oh help my aching, haunting being.
Let not me dwell in lands unseen.

In humble fervent prayer, I come.
Thy Victory won, Thy Victory won.

T'was Firmly Planted

T'was just a seed, but planted firm,
Took hold on solid ground.
The little root sprung up straight,
T'was strong, yet mellow sound.

Step by step it found its' way,
And firm it stood its' ground.
The seed deeply rooted set,
T'was planted in the mound.

T'when grown t' was firm and stout and green,
It's goal t' was heaven bound.
Growing strong in Grace and Beauty,
T'was 'Life' the seed had found.

"My Breath to 'You' Has't Flown"

Ah sweet love, my life now 'tis or'e.
Oh sweet rapture, warmth from the Golden core.

Ah sweet soul, fulfill, Thee, my aching heart.
Ner'e air'e from Thee, dear love, depart.

T'will mend the unforeseen shadow, woe.
When to Thee I come ner'e give I go.

Aw sweet gentle love in me take hold.
Ner'e turn aside Thy head, or speak O' cold.

Take my all and do it what Thee will.
Shine your 'light' upon my 'purple hill'.

Mold and make of me what air'e Ye might.
Give my Hill, sweet love, Thy everlasting light.

Ah sweet love, my breath to you hast flown.
Ner'e known death, ner'e be alone.

How Long Lord?

How long wilt thou stay away,
O' Lord my God, on High!
How long must I suffer, Lord,
To learn that thou art nigh.

God help me in my meager ways,
My strength from Thee I need.
Let not me go blind about,
Nor 'come a sordid seed.

Take my hand and heart, O' God,
Let ever me be thine.
Let not the bitter cup, O' God,
Take away the bread and wine!

O' God I am in misery,
When from you I stray.
Take me in Thy loving arms,
Keep my safe this day.

Peace He Gave Me

My sins are released in Jesus,
Because he died for me.
My sins are released in my Savior,
The Son of God, on Calvary.

I asked Him to forgive me,
And he heard my humble prayer.
Jesus forgives my sins and weakness,
Forgives other's, too, who care.

This I know, 'cause my heart's at peace,
I knows he loves us all.
I know Jesus cares for everyone,
Just listen and you'll hear His call.

My Humble Prayer

Help me, Lord, know the good,
The evil keep behind.
Help me, Lord, to walk the road,
Thou choose for all mankind.

Tarry not the obscene shore,
Ner'e tarry 'unknowingly' 'bout.
And if I tarry dusty walks,
Lift up Thy voice and shout!

Keep my pathway sandy loam,
And shores of whitened snow.
Keep my feet upon the ground,
These places that I go.

Let not the unforeseen hand,
Of evil take it's force.
Keep 'that' light a' shining, Lord,
In my straightway course.

Always guide and lead, thou, me,
Ner'e taste the bitter woe.

Keep that light a' glowing, Lord,
These places I must go.

Let me walk hand and hand,
With Thee, dear God, above.
Ner'e let me wonder lone, dear Lord,
Keep me safe in Jesus love.

In Thy Name Written?

Are you on the roll call,
In that book above?
Is your name written,
In letters, gold, with love?

Why?

Why be weak? And, why be bold?
Why cry your heart away? And,
Why be foolish and why be cold?
When 'Love' is here to stay!

Why care ye for earthly things?
When obtaining from no peace from it.
Why not wear heavenly wings?
And do your little bit.

Look not away from fellow man,
In trouble everywhere.
Give all the love you can,
Just do your little share.

Look not away from people,
Who work with you each day.
Put your eye on Heaven's steeple,
But do your bit today!

Help one another do ye good,
Become yourself er'e be strong.

Find grace 'neath Heaven's hood,
Eternal peace is long!

Keep your eye sunny peel,
And keep your eye on God.
Finding peace an even keel,
This blessed road do trod.

I Found

I found all in Christ my Lord,
And care not now to stray.
I know that Christ paid my debt,
And in Him I pray.

My sins are washed 'lily white',
My soul with God above.
My Savior is my 'guiding light',
Pure and sweet lasting love.

"I Nailed My Savior"

When I was a child, I used to wonder,
If God were really True.
Now I'm grown and Know His Love,
And will meet Him beyond the blue.

I wondered if he cared for me,
And knew that I was sad.
But I know he loves me,
And knowing this I'm glad.

I used to wonder why I was born,
And even this today I know.
For God made me in his own image,
A free will and love aglow.

He trusted me and warned me,
That from one tree not eat.
But I was a fool and listened not,
And suffered till I was beat.

And as the years passed me by,
And I was without my 'guide',

I was as a sinking ship,
Had I kept sinking, I'd had died.

But, one day when I was torn,
I turned my head to God.
I asked him then to help me,
Find the road to trod.

He heard my humble little prayer,
And his hand now guides my sail.
He told me of Christ his Son,
Who died from my single nail.

He told me Christ had died for me,
And that all I need to do.
Was "believe in Him" my sins now gone,
A friend indeed most true.

I opened my heart and no longer wonder,
If my God is real.
For in my heart are his words,
The Cross, the Golden Seal!

God

Yes, my God is real.
Yes, my God is true.

Yes, my God is love.
In Him I'm never blue.

God is My Strength

My strength comes from above,
For alone I cannot stand.
Without the constant watchful eye,
Nor the guiding hand.

I cannot weather all storms, alone.
Nor dusty roads I trod.
My strength comes from Thee 'mighty hand',
My Savior and my God.

'The Rainbow'

Let me see Thee 'rainbow', Lord,
The rain is heavy and long.
Keep my eye on the Rainbow, Lord,
Help me sing an Holy Song.

The rain keeps my thought astray, Lord,
And cluttered is my mind.
Help me see the Rainbow, Lord,
Eternal life, my find.

'Tis dark and drear' when clouds are here,
Oh, Lord, that Rainbow High.
Help me keep my eye peeled there,
For thou art ever nigh.

Do You Know Joey?

When Joey was a child,
He was so sweet and coy.
He was ever happy,
A darling little boy.

Joey went to school, now,
And learned so many things.
His teacher even taught him,
Many songs to sing.

Joey went to Sunday school,
And, even, there learned more.
About our loving Savior,
Who waites and Heaven's door.

Many years went along,
And Joey became a man.
He was busy working,
And away from church he ran.

A war had come, and Joey knew,
T'was foreign soil now seen.

Joey thought it was great,
The idea really keen!

It wasn't as Joey thought,
'Cause he really found great fear.
As Joey forgot that God and Christ,
Constantly are near!

He fear grew greater every day,
And, Joey, was scared to die.
He knew that Satan had him,
Then Joey began to cry.

Yes, Joey, no longer a tiny boy,
And tears came to his eyes.
But Joey then remembered,
The Christ, for him who died.

Joey knelt on the ground,
So wet, and cold and damp.
But, Joey's light was burning,
And found "oil" for his 'lamp'.

He remembered youth and Sunday school,
And all t'was taught him there.
He knew 'someone' died for him,
And new 'someone' does care.

He remembered the peace and consolation,
Found at that church, back home.
And wondered why he faltered,
And away from it did roam.

But Joey gave his heart that night,
To Christ our Savior, King.
And found himself 'reborn in light',
A new song now to sing.

Eternally

I gave my heart and soul to thee,
'Cause thou has't shown me love.
I give my heart and soul to thee,
My God, my Lord, above.

I give my heart and soul O' Lord,
I give my all to thee.
No longer lost, no longer torn,
Forever with thee eternally.

The "Lighted" Way

He taketh me from the blended path,
He leaded me His way.
He showed his light unto my soul,
He made the darkest day.

He consoled my heart and gave it peace,
He put smiles in the place of tears.
He gave me all the love he had,
And drove away my fears.

For at the Cross he gave his Son,
Who died to make us free.
What man on earth could give all this?
None! But, these, God giveth thee!!

He Knoweth me when others Not,
He speak with me night and day.
He Never goeth from my side,
He Knoweth in Him, that, I pray.

He Knoweth that ye love Him,
When in Jesus Name ye pray.
In your hearts he findeth peace,
Through Jesus who lighted the way.

Help Me Do Thine Will O' Lord

Help me do thine will O' Lord,
Lead me, guide me straight.
The narrow path is hard O' Lord,
Which leads to Heaven's gate.

Help me do thine will, O' Father,
Keep thine Hand on me.
Help me do thine will, O' God,
For Christ in Eternity.

Help me do thine will, O' Lord,
All my earthly days.
Yonder in the sunken field,
Lead others to your ways.

Thine will, now to be done, O' Lord,
For the love thou has't given me.
Let me do thine will, O' Father,
In Jesus Name to be.

"Give Me Thine Hand"

O' Lord and Savior, lest not though comest to me.
Give me thine hand, Lord, so that I can see.

Give me thy courage and strength from up above.
Keep me safe Lord, in Jesus gentle love.

Help me, guide me, lead me all thine ways.
Teach me in Jesus Name always, Lord, to pray.

"No Death in Thee"

Oh, sweet love, my life, now, 'tis 'oe'r.
O' sweet rapture, warmeth from the Golden core.

O' sweet soul, fulfill in Thee, my aching heart.
Ne're er'e from Thee, dear love, depart.

T'will mend the unforeseen, shadowed woe.
When to Thee I come, ne're I go.

O' sweet gentle love, on me take hold.
Ne're turn aside Thy Head, Ne're speak of 'cold'.

Take my all and do 'it' what Thee will.
Shine your 'light' upon my 'purple hill'.

Mold and make of me, what air'e Ye might.
Give my hill, sweet love, thy everlasting light.

Now, sweet love, my breath to you has't flown.
Ne're no death, ne're be alone.

Follow the Band

Have you met my Savior?
He's so kind and good.
He's the love we long for,
In our every mood.

Come meet my Savior,
He's The Truth, The Light.
Eternal Salvation,
He's worth 'that' fight.

Come meet him, now,
Come shake his hand.
Meet my sweet Savior,
Follow with Holy Band.

'Tis Gold

T'will watch the blue haze on the hill far away,
T'will see the blue, turn to gold.
T'will follow the gold beyond the hill,
The haze turned gold, tis near cold.

T'will linger beyond the hill far away,
T'will sing with glory and praise.
T'will hold the 'blue haze' close to my heart,
T'will onworldly, upwardly, gaze.

T'will know the Gold Light is lasting true life,
T'will cling to that 'golden crown'.
Ner'e let it slip by, ner'e will it die,
Ner'e fade, ner'e turn rusty nor brown.

The 'blue' is 'True Gold', for its color is pure,
The 'light' a' bright is found.
The trumpets of God's angels play holy tune,
Everlasting, everlasting, the sound.

In Closing

We hope you enjoyed this beautiful book and that you will tell others about this book so that they may find the peace and comfort these words bring to ones heart.

Our family is indebted to the loving care and dignity provided by the Hospice of the Sierras during the last months of her life.

On behalf of my mom, Justine Brockett, I have devoted my life to helping others improve the quality of their lives and their loved ones.

Join me

The Sandwich Crunch®

Speaker - TV, Radio & YouTube Host - Blog

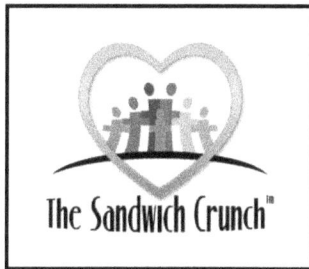

The Sandwich Crunch addresses issues and trends affecting the boomer, senior and elder populations. This creates a multi-generational crunch. Topics of focus include: aging, caregiving, patient advocacy, senior advocacy, retirement lifestyle, grief, death, and life celebrations. The programs presented provide pro-active solutions, strategies, support and resources that influence and transform individuals, families, communities, and businesses.

Join Us

Facebook.com - Bonnie B Kuhn
Facebook.com - The Sandwich Crunch
Linkedin.com - Bonnie (Brockett) Kuhn
YouTube.com/user/sandwichcrunch

Coming Summer 2014
The Sandwich Crunch Radio Show
Podomatic - The Sandwich Crunch

Looking for a Speaker for your business or organization?

Learn more about speaking presentations and
topics at:
www.BonnieKuhn.com/Presentations

Bonnie Brockett Kuhn, CSA
P. O. Box 3210 Arnold, CA 95223
Call: 209-730-6006 /209-595-9861
Email: Bonnie@BonnieKuhn.com